Fleece of Faith

FINDING GOD'S WILL

DR. TED O. PADGETT

Fleece of Faith

Copyright © 2021 by Dr. Ted O. Padgett. All rights reserved.

No part of this publication may be reproduced, stored in a retrieval system or transmitted in any way by any means, electronic, mechanical, photocopy, recording or otherwise without the prior permission of the author except as provided by USA copyright law.

The opinions expressed by the author are not necessarily those of URLink Print and Media.

1603 Capitol Ave., Suite 310 Cheyenne, Wyoming USA 82001
1-888-980-6523 | admin@urlinkpublishing.com

URLink Print and Media is committed to excellence in the publishing industry.

Book design copyright © 2021 by URLink Print and Media. All rights reserved.

Published in the United States of America

Library of Congress Control Number: 2021903080
ISBN 978-1-64753-692-3 (Paperback)
ISBN 978-1-64753-693-0 (Digital)

25.01.21

Contents

Words From The Author 7
Chapter 1: Fleecing God With Faith Dealing With The
Doubters 11
Chapter 2: Setting Up The Story 16
Chapter 3: Fleecing God With Faith
Sailor And Salvation (1960–1965) 20
Chapter 4: College Choice (1965–1969) 24
Chapter 5: Education And Evangelism (1969-1973) 27
Chapter 6: Divine Direction (1973–1975) 32
Chapter 7: Faith Fumble (1975–1979) 35
Chapter 8: God's Gunslinger (1979–1997) 39
Chapter 9: Building And Battling (1997–2012) 43
Chapter 10: Be Believing (2012–2018) 48
Notes 53
Bibliography 55

WORDS FROM THE AUTHOR

My reason for writing this book concerning the *fleece* is to show that it can be used for a person called by God for a mission or ministry. Too many scholars and skeptics say it is not to be used. However, it is in the Bible, and Gideon did use it for this very purpose (Judges 6:36-40).

My main thesis of this book is to show there are biblical principles shown for using the "fleece of faith" that must be applied. By my life's major fleeces, I will explain how God directly answered my "fleeces of faith."

This book is written entirely to show and prove without a doubt that the "fleece of faith" works if the correct biblical principles of faith are used and applied (Hebrews 11:6).

Dr. Ted O. Padgett
B.A., M.DIV., D.MIN.
July 2018

So Gideon said to God, "If you will save Israel by my hand as you have said to me, I will put a fleece on the threshing floor; if there is dew on the fleece only, and if it is dry on all the ground, then I shall know that you will save Israel by my hand, as you have said." And it was so, when he rose early the next morning and squeezed the fleece together, he wrung the dew out of the fleece a bowlful of water. Then Gideon said to God,

"Do not be angry with me, but let me speak just once more: let me test, I pray, just once more with the fleece; let it now be dry only on the fleece, but on all the ground let there be dew:"

And God did so that night. It was dry on the fleece only, but there was dew on all the ground.

- Judges 6:36-40, NKJV

To my wife, Anne Corley Padgett, "who everyone knows that you are a woman of virtue, excellence, and beauty" Ruth 3:11 (NASV), and that I am the most blessed among men. Your special love for me has always been my treasure and joy in life. You are my greatest gift and love sent from God.

CHAPTER 1

FLEECING GOD WITH FAITH
Dealing with the Doubters

So, Gideon laid out a fleece before God to be sure of his will...

-Judges 6:36-40, RSV

As I found out in my Bible classes in college and later in my seminary studies, "putting out a fleece before God" is a foolish thing to do, according to my professors of Bible studies for ministry. They were all bigtime doubters of the fleece.

The doubters say that using a "fleece" to find God's will is a very immature spiritual thing to do for a believer. They say to use a "fleece" to find God's will is a very foolish and very silly act on the part of a believer. However, I am firmly convicted and spiritually convinced that it is a true act of faith to use a fleece before God to find his will. Gideon did certainly use a fleece, as the Bible records in Judges 6:36–40. The major fleeces of my life, as shown in the later chapters, will show the use of the "fleece" as a way of finding God's will.

Dr. John MacArthur in his book, Found: God's will, argues against the fleece for anyone seeking God's divine will. He says, "If you are a Spirit filled, sanctified (means: set apart for God, or dedicated to God), submissive to God's will and authority, and willing to suffer for Christ in a hostile world, then, God will be shaping and forming His desires in our lives. We will not need a method such as the fleece."[1]

Yes, those are all facts of faith about knowing and finding God's will. But it does not mean the "fleece of faith" cannot be used to find God's perfect will for your life! The fleece is truly a fact of faith that was used in the Bible by Gideon and can be used to determine God's perfect will.

Dr. Eric J. Bargerhuff says, "Get rid of the fleece. Ditch the pursuit of signs in the sky or reading into situations what ought not to be read into for the purposes of finding God's will. Desiring these kinds of discernment tactics should be a red flag, reminding us we are not walking with God as close enough to have Him shape the desires of our hearts for his will."[2]

All what Dr. Bargerhuff says is somewhat truthful for theological interpretation, however, it does not disprove the "fleece of faith" just because he feels the way he believes. The fleece for finding God's will is in the Bible, if you believe it!

Dr. W. Gary Phillips says, "Those who take Gideon's request for a fleece as a model for divine guidance are ill-advised. Gideon's request was not an expression of faith, but a questioning of God's promises and power."[3]

Yes, it may be true that Gideon had concerns but he was not in doubt about God's power or *his word*. It seems to me that Gideon was really trying to determine God's *perfect will* in the situation.[4]

My purpose and central thesis of this book is to show the Bible truth of the fleece request. Remember, God created everything and is in control of all things, and we can write that over the life of the child of God and God's will for their life (Romans 8:28).

Gideon was aware that he was asking in disbelief and in partial rebellion to God's mission for him, which states, "God do not be angry with me" (Judges 6:39).

Remember that Gideon was unsure and unstable about the great task God had called him to do. He was trying to be sure and certain of God's perfect will for his life, and he used the "fleece of faith" to do so!

Now in dealing with doubters, skeptics, and critics, we must keep in mind they are using a very shallow view of the fleece. Again, my purpose is to show that our Great Almighty God hears and does answer our faithful prayers to Him, and yes, the fleece of faith! God hears and answers the "fleece of faith" given to him by one of his called servants who is earnestly and honestly seeking to determine God's perfect will for a called mission task or ministry. He may already know God's will for his life. However, he needs to make sure it is God's will and not his own personal desire in the situation.

Dr. W. W. Wiersbe, one of my personal favorite Bible scholars who is very conservative on Biblical interpretation, does not favor using the "fleece of faith" in seeking God's will in a matter. He states that the term "putting out the fleece" is a familiar one in religious circles. It means asking God to guide us in a decision by fulfilling some conditions that we lay down before Him.

Then he says, "In my own personal pastoral ministry, I have met all kinds of people who have gotten themselves into trouble using the fleece. Putting out the fleece is not a good Biblical method for determining the Will of God."[5]

Too many professors and so-called Bible scholars say their use of the "fleece" approach is used by people who do not have a real deep-rooted faith relationship with God. I completely disagree with them and believe just the opposite that Gideon and others who use the "fleece of faith" method have a very deep rooted faith in God and His word! They also have a devoted and close relationship with Him.

The doubters, skeptics, and critics say that Gideon's request to God in Judges 6:36–37 shows that Gideon already knew God's will for him. Of course, Gideon did ask God twice to affirm his will to him. But if you notice, God did answer his faith fleece laid out. God knows the heart of his servants. (1 Samuel 16:7).

Yes, there is the fact of some disbelief on the part of Gideon and others who used the fleece to seek God's will for sure. However, they were uncertain and really wanted to be sure.[6]

There are some definite principles and steps for using the "fleece of faith" for finding God's will. Next, we will explain principles and steps that you must use in laying out a fleece before God

Important: Principles and Steps for

Using the Fleece of Faith

1. *Step one:* A person who has been called and/or directed by God for a certain mission or ministry can lay a fleece out before God to find God's *perfect will* in the situation.
2. *Step two:* The person must prayerfully lay out certain conditions that will show God's will and his direction. Example, if a person feels God is leading and directing them to a certain seminary for ministry training, and they are not certain as was my situation, their "fleece of faith" could be for God to have a person to directly and purposefully talk to them about going to seminary, and to a particular seminary for ministry training. Also, a certain time factor must be set for the answer to happen.
3. *Step three*: The facts that have been laid out before God in the "fleece of faith" must not be shared with anyone, unless it is a person's soulmate in marriage like wife, and/or at times, a parent or mentor in life such as a pastor. But they are to make sure they tell no one or even speak of it until the time of the fleece has been fulfilled.
4. *Step four:* The fleece laid out before God must be in fact completely followed as God has answered it as either yes or no. You must, by faith follow God's will, and answer in the matter as directed by God for his will.

Example: if you asked God to show you what Theological Seminary you should attend and he directly and divinely answers, you then are bound by your fleece of faith to follow God's direction. Therefore, it is called a "fleece of faith" (Hebrews 11:6). It takes a completely faithful person to God's answer. Later chapters of this book will give some exact examples of my life's personal fleeces laid out before God for his will. Fifty years of following my God and using the "fleece of faith should prove that the fleece does work. It should disprove the skeptic and doubters in their disbelief of God's word and teaching.

My utmost desire and prayer for this book is that God will get the glory for all he has done, and is doing in my life and the life of our family! No way do I want to glorify myself, but it has been my life with God's leading me by the "fleece of faith". Now, continue reading in the following chapters as to how God used the faith principles and steps of the "fleece of faith."[7]

CHAPTER 2

Setting Up the Story

So, Gideon laid out a fleece before God to be sure of his will.

- Judges 6:36-40, RSV

How and why I used the "fleece of faith" will be more fully explained in this chapter! To get where we're going, we must start where we came from. This is why this chapter is called "Setting Up the Story" for the use of putting forth a fleece before God.

The "fleece of faith" determines God's *perfect will* in a matter and it helps in being completely sure of God's will (Judges 6:36-40).

Gideon was a man who wanted to be certain of God's will and laid out the fleece before God. Just as Gideon's life had shaped him to be used by God, so are all the people God calls to ministries and/or missions for his kingdom's glory. Gideon was such a man of faith who wanted to know for certain.[8]

Our life is the foundation that our faith is eventually built upon. Remember, where you are now is a direct result of where you came from! And particularly in the choices we make in our life's journey. It's our background and experiences that builds the character and integrity of our personal life before God and with people.

My story background was really not the best of stories, though it did mold and prepare me for the time when God truly became my own personal Lord and savior. It was my sixth birthday and my mother had given me a party with my friends and family. This is the only birthday party I had until my fiftieth birthday when my three daughters gave me a surprise party.[9]

I am not trying to have a poor me "pity party". I am just stating some minor details and facts of my life! The year was 1948 and it was nice time in America. World War II was over in 1945 and my dad had come home from the war. He was an Army Airborne Paratrooper who had served in North Africa and Italy. The people of America were grateful to all the veterans, and above all, to God for a time of peace.

My mother and daddy were the typical worldly young married couple of those post-World War II years! My mother was only sixteen when she married my daddy who was nineteen at that time. Neither of them were into church and/or the Christian life behavior, though both professed to be!

There were times when we would go to church together. However, most of my times were with my mother. When I was a baby, I was christened and later when I was about eight years old, I was sprinkled.

Then at age twelve, I was baptized in a pond by complete emersion!

(Note that with all these different times and types of believer's baptism, I was *not* saved or Born Again as a real believer in Jesus Christ (John 3:1-16).[10]

My six to eleven years were filled with sad memories of my daddy and mother "fussing and cussing and drinking and going to places for dancing and partying. I remember too many times of being put on the backseat of the car with a blanket and pillow to wait for my mother and daddy while they were inside a nightclub, to dance and get drunk! Many times, this went way up into the late-night hours. I can still see in my mind's memory the giant red neon sign on the top of the nightclub that read *El Roco Club.*

During those times, my life was very difficult and there was really no reason to go into all those days of sadness. Most of those stories are recorded in my autobiography entitled "Changed."

In January 1954, I had just turned eleven in December when my mother was tragically killed in an automobile wreck! A drunk driver ran a red stop light and "T-boned" her on the driver's side killing her instantly at the very young age of twenty-eight years.

It was a drastic time in my life. I was thinking at that time that my mother and daddy were beginning to get along happily together.

I began to live with my grandmother at this time. I always called her mama lovingly. After my mother's death, I lived with my grandmother until the age of seventeen when I joined the Navy.

Mama was one of the best of people and she truly showed forth the real Christ-like spirit and behavior. She was a big giant of a woman standing six feet and three inches tall and very big-boned but not fat! She was a very dedicated believer and certainly did her best to raise me accordingly.

(Note: she shared with me the truth that we had two ordained ministers in our family tree on her side of the family.)

The years of my life after my mother's tragic death were filled with hate and rebellion in school, in sports, and in my life events. I seemed to be trying to find the real meaning and answer of life. (Note: These were my years eleven through seventeen).[11]

Fast forward to the spring of 1960. I was seventeen when I joined the U.S. Navy. This was one of God's biggest plans in my life's journey. The biggest and best event of my life happened to me when I met my soon-to-be wife at the age of fourteen.[12]

She was just thirteen years old. We were both born on December 7, except that I am a year older. At first sight, I fell in love with this beautiful blue-eyed blonde. She was an adventurous girl full of life! Really, it was like the old saying "She had me with one hello"! I could never get over this girl. By the way, she was definitely *God's divine will* for my life (Genesis 24:1-67).

Now, in this book, I am not telling the whole story of our life as teenagers in the wonderful 1960s or about our lives in general. That will be a completely different book-our autobiography. (See: *Changed* written by Ted O. Padgett published in 2019). This present book is only about the fleece of God in our life.

Fast-forward until Anne and I were married. I was in the Navy, and we were living in San Diego, California. My wife was a Christian believer and had joined the First Baptist Church of San Diego. She attended the Young Marrieds' Department and was growing in her faith. I was stationed on a ship and was out to sea from Monday through Friday of most weeks. When we came in to dock, I'd get to go home over the weekend and be with her.

At first, I would not go to church with my wife. But soon after we had our first baby, a son named Ted Jr., I started attending church. In my mind, I was saying I wanted to be a good daddy for my son and guide my family in the right way.

As we attended church, I soon realized God was really convicting me that I was lost, and not a saved believer! During that time, I was miserable and just *could not go t*o church without feeling the preacher and God were talking to me in the sermon message! That is a real Holy Spirit conviction (John 16:7-11).

It wasn't long before I got *saved* and that is when my whole life *changed (*2 Corinthians 5:17). As the Bible states, "When you are changed, you've been changed."

I truly love the Bible Scripture that says "God sees the heart of man, but man sees the outside appearance" (Samuel 16:7).

Now in those early days of my salvation and believer's baptism, God mentored me spiritually by a wonderful Bible teacher. He taught the Young Marrieds Sunday School class and would become a lifelong friend. It was this man and also my pastor during this time of my life who shared with me and directed me to Gideon's "fleece of faith," which Gideon used to make sure of God's will.[13]

It was my heart's desire to find God's will for my life and it seemed to me that God wanted me to go into the Gospel Ministry but I did not know for sure about God's will. The act of putting a "fleece of faith" before God to direct my life for his will would be an ongoing part of the rest of my life's spiritual journey with God. The fleece would be an important act for me to ensure God's perfect will for divine direction in my life. It's all for his glory!

Now read on in the following chapters of this book about those major "fleeces of faith" in our life's journey for God's will and his glory!

CHAPTER 3

FLEECING GOD WITH FAITH
Sailor and Salvation
(1960–1965)

Fleecing God with faith sounds like we mean we can trick God into doing what we want. Mainly because the word *fleece* means by street language "to take advantage of by means of trickery methods". But as we have explained in the earlier chapter, it is a method of laying before God a *divine difficulty* where you are not certain of his will in the situation.

"Fleecing God with faith" began as a way for me to know and to find God's will for my life's journey! After joining the Navy in March of 1960, I went to San Diego Naval Training Center for boot camp training. It was a time of physical fitness training to the extreme and plenty of marching and rifle drills. This was twelve weeks' time of training from April through the last of June.

In the summer of 1961, about one and a half years after my boot camp and a year of training in the Naval Radar Training Center, which was located at Treasure Island, California in the Bay of San Francisco, I was given two weeks' leave. I came back home for the first time since the day I joined the Navy in March of 1960. It was now August 1961.

My purpose was to ask my childhood sweetheart, Anne Corley, to marry me! My plan was to surprise her. She did not know I was coming home. Remember it was summer time in August of 1961 and she was, on that day, returning from her week at High School Band Camp.

Anne played the flute and was soon to begin her senior year of high school and was seventeen years old. I surprised her by meeting the band bus when she returned. It was a big surprise for her! A few days later, we decided to elope and get married. The years of our young days of marriage are told in more detail in our autobiography entitled *Changed*.

It was in March 1965 that I became a Born Again believer of Jesus Christ. My journey with God after salvation began to move very fast. I began growing as a new baby in Jesus Christ, our Lord.

My journey with God began to change my life's goals from wanting to have a military career to doing and being what God wanted for me. I was truly and earnestly seeking God's will.

Fast forward to the summer of 1967. When I was in the middle of the Viet Nam War, it was my fourth time to be in the Tonkin Gulf, China Sea just off the coast of Viet Nam. Most of the Navy ships went over for six to ten months. It was called Wespac Cruise.

The Naval ships were in support of the war and the troops on the ground in Viet Nam. We were there for ten months of our time at Wespac Cruise

By this time, I was an E-6, Radar Air-Intercept Controller Operations Specialist serving as a Combat Controller. Many times, the helicopter would take us from ship to shore to do our work in support of the inland troops. As stated, it was the summer of 1967 and I found myself inland in Viet Nam in support of the troops as a *combat air controller* for the troops northeast of our site on Monkey Mountain, a Marine Battery position. It was there that my first major fleece was laid out before God.

Feeling that God was calling me into his ministry for quite some time, I needed to find God's perfect will for my life. So I laid out my first major "fleece of faith" before him to determine his divine will and purpose.

Knowing that I had not gone to college at this time in my life, and that I would need it and the seminary if I were to undergo training for ministry, I laid out my first major fleece before God for his *perfect will* for me.

Note: My first major fleece, "Sailor and Salvation"

My "fleece of faith" to God was simply, "God if you are really calling me into ministry then send orders for me to have shore duty at home in San Diego with my wife. Then I will know you want me to get out of the Navy and finish my studies for the Gospel Ministry".

This was my simple "fleece of faith" to God.

Remember we were in the middle of the Tonkin Gulf and I was on Monkey Mountain on Viet Nam soil when I prayed and laid out this first fleece to God. Nobody was getting orders back to the United States from the Viet Nam conflict. But the answer to my fleece came within days. God answered!

Orders came in for me to be *immediately* transferred back to San Diego to the Naval Instructor's School for training. This was where my wife and home were! It was God's mighty miracle directly answering my "fleece of faith".

The next thing that happened after the orders came was me being transferred from my ship by *helo to* Saigon, Viet Nam to then be sent to Manila, and then be sent back to the United States. What a joy and praise to God to be home with my wife and little son and daughter, Ted Jr. and Deanna.

There was no doubt in my mind that God directly and divinely answered my prayer "fleece of faith". This was truly the beginning of my simple faith of just believing and following God for my life's journey. God knew me and had divinely called me into his Gospel Ministry.

During this time of shore-duty in San Diego, God was still showing his mighty power and miracles in my life, confirming the "fleece of faith" that showed he had called me into ministry. After arriving in San Diego for training at the Naval Instructor's School, I saw God at work in my life preparing me for his Gospel Ministry For example, nobody was ever assigned permanent duty at the Instructor's School as part of the training staff. I was selected by the school's staff to become a staff instructor. It was by the grades I made and my teaching performance in the twelve-week school.

By God's will and divine providence, I was selected to become part of the teaching staff. This meant our family would not have to relocate to some other area, and that I could be home more.

During my two years at the Instructor's School, it gave me time to be more involved at my home church where I was saved and had spiritual mentors at the F.B.C. of San Diego, California. It gave me time to attend evening classes at Mesa College where I completed a full year's classes.

CHAPTER 4

College Choice
(1965–1969)

My second major "fleece of faith" was all about going to college and where God wanted me to go for my first major formal college educational degree. It was about the college choice God wanted me to attend.

Our family was happily living in San Diego, California where I was serving on the staff of the U.S. Navy's Instructor's School. It was a great few years in our life for our family to grow in our faith in the Lord Jesus Christ and in being a real family together. By this year of 1967, we had bought our first house.

Those years were used for preparation of God's future full-time ministry. Every minute of not being on my military duty was used to enjoy my stay with my family while going to college at night.

It was in the fall of 1968 and the spring of 1969 that I was trying to find out which college to attend. I would be getting out of the Navy in November of 1969.

By the spring of 1969, my home church, F.B.C. of San Diego, ordained me as a Deacon and officially licensed me to the Gospel Ministry. It was a great time being used in my home church and around the San Diego area mostly as a youth preacher. It was a time of learning to preach the Gospel and to personally grow in my faith. Knowing I needed to decide on where God wanted me to go to college, my second major "fleece of faith" was laid before God for him to guide and direct me. I wanted his divine will. Again, it was the spring of 1969.

Knowing many people in the San Diego area and being used by God to preach, I was an Interim Pastor for a church in the area and quite often my pastor used me to preach and to teach. It was my personal choice to stay in the Southern California area for college.[14]

My pastor at this time had tried to influence me to go to Riverside Baptist College in Riverside, California just north of San Diego. He was a member of the Board of Directors there. He said the school had a great Bible and Religion Department for me to major in Bible.

Coming from South Carolina, we had been in San Diego for nine years. Our home was South Carolina and we wanted to be back toward the East Coast for college training. But above all, we wanted God's perfect will!

We began looking for schools again toward the Carolinas. After getting college catalogs from many schools and after reviewing their curriculum, we narrowed our choices down to five schools. Riverside College was one of the five. We began to constantly pray for God's direction daily. It was a very serious time in our lives and I was unsure and confused about my choice much like Gideon in Judges 6:36-40.

It was now that my second "fleece of faith" was laid before God to find his *perfect will* in the matter![15]

Second Major Fleece of Faith: College Choice

My simple "fleece of faith" to God was the following:

"God, please show me which college you want me to attend after getting out of the Navy in November this year 1969. Show me what school you want me to attend before July of this year. Please have someone inform me by then that you were leading them to encourage me to go to a certain college. If no one does this by July, I will go to Riverside College which is my choice."[16]

My "fleece of faith" may seem silly and even ridiculous to the skeptics and doubters. However, my simple faith and trust in God would be put to the test. My God knew I was sincerely seeking his divine will and providence in the matter (Hebrews 11:6).

After setting the above fleece, the second one of my life to this point, prayer had become a continuous part of my daily activities! It was the spring of 1969 when the fleece was laid before God. About three months before July 1969, I needed God to show me which of the five schools he wanted me to attend.

Remember, someone had to talk to me and say that God had led them to encourage me to attend a certain college by July 1969 or else, we would stay in San Diego area and attend my personal choice.

As always, "God showed up!" He showed up in a mighty way, as he does, in answering my fleece! It was on a Sunday afternoon, a few days before my fleece would run out of the time limit set. A phone call came to me from Rock Hill, South Carolina. Since it was Sunday afternoon, we were all down taking a restful nap as part of our custom. A phone call came from my brother-in-law, Howard Craft.

By the way, we were not really that close at this time in our life and he knew nothing about a "fleece" or what we were planning to do.

He called me saying, "Today, in our church worship service, we had a small singing group from a college up in Tennessee, named Carson-Newnan College. It is very close to Knoxville, and they were a great spiritual singing group. During the time they were singing, God impressed me to call you and to encourage you to go to this college. I am only calling to obey God." That was Howard's phone call verbatim.

Well, hallelujah and to God be the glory! God showed up mightily as he had already done for me in my first major "fleece of faith"! It was a divine answer to my fleece! You must realize this was a mighty miraculous act and answer from God. At this time in my life of the year 1969, I had never even been to Tennessee! However, Carson-Newnan College was, in fact, one of the five colleges we were considering.

Now we were sure about God's divine will for the place where we will go to college and where we will move in November of that year, after getting out of the Navy. God had answered, and we knew his will for which college to attend.

CHAPTER 5

Education and Evangelism
(1969-1973)

It was November of 1969, a week before Thanksgiving Day, and I had just gotten out of the U.S. Navy after nine and a half years of active duty. We were now moving from San Diego, California, to a small college town just north of Knoxville, Tennessee. This would be a move from one side of the United States to the other. God had shown us this was the college he wanted me to attend.

Some of the events that took place had to have God's hand in them. Let me share a few of them to give God the glory. By the way, to give God glory is my purpose in this whole book's story. Only God could have done what happened to get us to college for the spring semester of 1970, which started in January.

In November 1969 when our little family arrived in Tennessee, it was our first time to be in that state. It was like a culture shock from our life in San Diego, California. But as God led us to Tennessee, it had become our chosen state that we would call *home* for the rest of our family's lives! The town we now lived in only had one stop light. It was a small little college town. It was so perfect for our little family.

As we arrived, we figured God had it all set up for us. But upon arriving, we found that there was no college housing available for us to move into. After hours of searching, the people in charge of the college housing did find us a place to live for the first semester which would run for six months.

By then, they thought we could move on campus into the college housing. Again, we could see God's hand in all that was happening in every step we took (Psalm 37:23).

As a matter of fact, the house they put us in for the first semester to live was a missionary's home. It was a wonderful house. Many interesting events took place in these early days of college. These events are more detailed in the book *Changed*.

After settling into the new schedule of college life, God began giving me many opportunities to preach the Gospel in the very small churches all around the East Tennessee area on the weekends. God used me every Sunday to preach somewhere after the first few weeks of moving to Tennessee! It was the providential hand of God over my life and I truly believe it was, because I did trust and follow God's answer to my fleece for college direction!

My third major fleece for my life came within the next year of being in college. It was in my first full-time pastorate that this third

"fleece of faith" would take place. The first time that I pastored a church was a very wonderful time. The people were very loving and the kind of people who follow their pastor's leadership. Our family was truly blessed by this first church.

We were very near the college that I was attending full-time.

Wow, we had such a big and beautiful church-owned pastorium to live in. We felt so loved by the people and so very blessed by God.

God really blessed my ministry in this first church pastorate.

The church had record numbers of believers being baptized and many others were joining the membership. Before long, the little church was overcrowded for Sunday's worship! Even the little balcony was full. Chairs were placed in the back and down the aisles. It was the mighty wonderful blessings of God upon our ministry.

It was in the midst of all these blessings that my next fleece would be laid before God. The reason for my "fleece of faith" was because I felt God wanted me to go into full-time evangelism. At this time, I had only been at the church for two years.

People from many places were asking me to come and preach revivals, and even other opportunities to speak at evangelism conferences. One of my concerns was, the church where I was pastoring full-time only allowed me to be gone for two weeks a year which meant I could not do any revivals and have a family vacation. This situation brought forth my reason to put my next "fleece of faith" before God to find his perfect and divine direction. Even though God was using me mightily in this first pastorate, my soul was burning with the "fires of evangelism" and to be in full time vocational evangelism. So my desire was to preach revivals, and to witness to the lost and dying unbeliever.

Not sure of God's will in this matter, or if it was just all my own selfish desire. My "fleece of faith" was laid before God for his will to be shown to me! This was my fleece laid out before God:

"God, if you want me to go into full-time evangelism and resign my present position as a pastor, then send me ten revival opportunities before Easter Sunday."

This was laid out before God in late January 1972. At this time, I had no revivals scheduled, and it would be three months before Easter Sunday of the year 1972.

Remember, no one but my wife and I, and God, knew about this "fleece of faith" laid before God to determine his will! We, our family, were extremely happy and satisfied in this pastorate plus the blessings of God were very obvious to everyone.

There was not even a hint that I may resign. The "fires of evangelism" were burning in my soul to be a full-time Evangelist! It was like the fire in the Prophet Jeremiah's soul recorded in the Bible in the Book of Jeremiah found in Chapter 20.

Now it was a time to constantly pray and to see how God's *perfect will w*ould be answered for my life. Again, it all would depend on a "fleece of faith" laid before God in faith. The time you are waiting for your fleece to be answered is a time of real spiritual praying and reading and studying God's Holy Word while you continue your present ministry and activities.

Once again, God answered in his mighty and miraculous way! I counted the revivals that came in for me to lead, one by one. Then the tenth one came about two weeks before Easter Sunday! Hallelujah and praise the Lord my God!

I was sure of his will for my life, in my mind, without a doubt!

It was God's divine will at this time in my life to go into full-time Evangelism. It meant I would have to resign as the pastor of the people and the place I'd grown to love very much. *But* I was sure God had divinely and directly answered my "fleece of faith"!

It was a time of tears and a time of joy for my family, and for the church family. On Easter Sunday 1972, I resigned as pastor and began my ministry in full-time evangelism. It became a time of really leaning on God as he opened doors of ministry and for us to ask him to provide for our daily needs.

(Note: We went into evangelism without any money in the bank, and no people to help us financially.)

I kept telling my wife and family that "Where God guides, God provides" and we would start a life-long act of claiming the scripture promise in Philippians 4:19, which states, "Your God will supply all your needs, according to his riches in glory."

Remember we were completely trusting in God to lead us and to take care of our needs as a family. I was to graduate from college in June 1972, just a few months after going into full-time Evangelism. We had to move out of the beautiful Pastorium, and into a very small old farm house we found, to rent in a nearby community. We knew things always work out if you follow God's will for your life.

The first year in Evangelism, God gave me twenty revivals. It was twice the amount I had asked for and, of course, those revival opportunities brought in more revivals. In fact, it seemed I was too busy to keep pace with all the ministry opportunities that God was giving me.

(Note: Financially, it was very hard for us but in some way we always made it month-by-month.) Some churches did not give us much in their *love offering*, while others seemed to make up for the other small offerings! Never in my life had I set a certain amount that a church must give for me to come for a revival.

Yes, at times the offerings given were like the *widow's mites* while at other times there would be a large offering given to me. Keep in mind, I never talked about money. It seemed to me that my God called me into full-time evangelism, and I was going to trust him. We always paid the bills and had all we needed. God had said, "He would take care of our *needs,* not our *greed."* He did, and he will!

It is very important to remember the true Biblical saying, "Where God guides, God always provides"! Three months into full time evangelism, we found out we were going to be blessed with another baby!

It would be seven years since our last baby was born and wow, *our God surprises in many ways*! This baby would always be our little evangelism baby. In those days of year 1972, we did not know what the baby's gender would be until the delivery. So we were not sure if our new baby would be a boy or girl but we had a name ready for either gender!

The baby—our "evangelism baby"—was a precious girl! We named her Terena! She has been a real joy to our life. Oh, speaking of finances just a little bit ago, let me tell you that we had no hospital and/or medical insurance at the time of her birth and I went straight to the hospital's financial office with the week's revival *love offering* and paid for her delivery. It was just the right amount of revival offering to pay our debt!

So much more, I'd like to share with you about our days in Evangelism as we were following God's will through his answer of the "fleece of faith" but this is a book on the "fleece of faith" and "how to find God's will"!

Now let's move on to my next and fourth "fleece of faith" in finding God's will for my life. It will be in chapter six.

CHAPTER 6

Divine Direction
(1973–1975)

It was the spring of 1973, and I was in the process of a series of revivals and evangelism conferences that would take me from the east coast South Carolina, to west coast California. These opportunities would be back-to-back, without me having a chance to return home to be with my family for nine straight weeks! This was my first longtime of being away on the "revival trail."

It would be that during this long series of revivals that God put another divine directional plan in my soul and in my heart. I felt completely happy in full-time evangelism but my soul was being burdened again in another direction by God. Even though I had graduated from college with my bachelor's degree, I was now feeling led toward more education via theological seminary training.

Until now, I felt I had enough schooling and theological training to be an effective minister. My college bachelor's degree was a double major in Bible and History with two years of New Testament Greek as my language with a minor in Meteorology.

Now with this spiritual conviction in my heart and soul, I laid out my fourth major "fleece of faith" before God for his will and divine direction for my life. My fleece was this:

"God if you are leading me to go to seminary then within the next seven days, have someone write me a letter encouraging me to go to seminary for more Theological training. Also, on the same day, have someone talk personally to me about going to a certain seminary for more training. God, have both things happen on the same day by two different people. Have this happen within the next seven days."

Again, this was my simple "fleece of faith" laid out before God for his divine direction. I knew God had already guided and directed me at other major crossroads in my life at times when I was unsure and uncertain about his perfect will for me.

It was as Gideon in Judges 6:36-40. Gideon wanted to be certain of God's will. This is when a person can lay out a fleece to God.

The spirituals principles and steps for placing a fleece before God have been given in an earlier chapter (Chapter 1, "Dealing with the Doubters").

Keep in mind that each time you lay a "fleece of faith" before God, it is to be a time of constant prayer and spiritual meditation. Acts 17:26, Jeremiah 29:11, Psalm 37:5, and Proverbs 16:3 say, "God has a plan and determines the events according to his will" (Paraphrased, NRSV). Also, there are certainly many, many more scriptures. God certainly guides and directs the events of his creations for his purpose and his will.

God did answer my "fleece of faith" in a mighty and miraculous way. It took place like this: Because of the long time in the past weeks of revivals, my little Volkswagen "bug" needed to be taken to the dealership for servicing and oil change. I had bought it in our college days the year before. It was 1972 VW.

The car dealership was near our college and small town.

Remember that we still lived in the little "farm house" we were renting. After putting my car in for servicing, I decided to walk around and go get a cup of coffee. As I was walking, someone called out my name and came over to me. It was a young man, a youth minister at a nearby church. We walked down the street together to a coffee shop to have a cup and talk.

As we sat there drinking our coffee, the old friend began to share with me that he'd just finished going to seminary and he thought I'd enjoy going too. He encouraged me to go to the seminary he had attended which is the Southwestern Baptist Theological Seminary in Fort Worth, Texas. He kept saying it was the best place for me to attend seminary!

As I sat there, I knew that this was a "divine encounter" as part of the answer to the "fleece of faith" laid out before God seeking his will. When I got home, my wife said there was a letter for me that had come from San Diego, California.

Wow, the two parts to my fleece had been answered exactly as I had laid it out before God! That same day, a letter came for me and someone different had personally talked with me about going to seminary. Hallelujah and praise the Lord because God again answered one of my prayer "fleeces of faith"! The skeptics and the doubters can make fun and laugh at using the fleece but my God hears and answers the seeking faithful heart (Psalm 37:5, Proverbs 16:3)

CHAPTER 7

Faith Fumble
(1975–1979)

It was May 1973 and God had led us to Southwestern Baptist Theological Seminary in Fort Worth, Texas. After moving from Tennessee to our new home in Texas, I registered for the two summer school semesters starting in June through August. It was a busy summer as were the next few years in seminary training for my master's degree.

The title of this chapter is "Faith Fumble" because when playing football, fumble happens when you drop the ball or it can just mean you made a mistake! As you will see in this chapter, as it always happens to so many people striving to live for God, we'll fumble in our faith which means we will make mistakes in our journey of faith.

Some can just fumble in their faith because they have "burned out" with all the daily pressures of family, studies, and ministry. Others are simply very careless and they fumble because they are not careful to remember the devil's tactics against the children of God (1 Peter 5:8).

Actually, my "faith fumble" comes later in this chapter. It is more because of not being careful about the devil's attacks and his tactics. Truly, my fumble was also because of flat "burnout" in ministry and in my patience with the sheep God had given me to shepherd—that is, to be their pastor.

So let's move quickly through my seminary study days until the last few years. In May 1974, God blessed us with another baby girl Letitia! Her name means *happine*ss and she surely brought us much joy and happiness when she was born in Mexia, Texas. It was there in Mexia that I had a sort of large church to pastor for me to be a seminary student! We all lived there, and I drove over one hundred miles one way to Fort Worth for semi-nary classes at 8:00 a.m. for three times a week and got back home around 6:00 p.m. on those days.

To say the least, it was a very busy and hard time in our family's lives. It was our family that kept me going hard to get my studies completed. Oh, don't forget, I knew God's will was for me to get my Master of Divinity degree.

We were now a family of six. My wife and I, my son Ted Junior, and my three daughters—Deanna, Terena, and Letitia. They were then and are now my great treasures and joy of life. As I approached seminary graduation in May 1975, my next major fleece came in my life. It was my fifth major fleece for my life's journey.

Before getting into this fleece of faith, let me set the stage of the setting as to how it came about. We had left the Mexia, Texas Pastorate to become pastor of a church in Forth Worth, Texas, one year before I was to graduate from seminary. It certainly was a great help for our family to be closer to the seminary and for me in my efforts in my studies.

Six months after my graduation from seminary, a pulpit committee of six people came to hear me preach and interview me to become their pastor. The committee had flown down in a private airplane from a city close to St. Louis. This was a surprise and shock to me and my family, but as always, my only choice was to seek God's perfect will in the situation. This is the setting for this fleece of faith, my fifth major fleece!

Some side bar notes must be given for you to understand a few facts. Many major events had happened in our lives since the last fleece was laid before God. They were big decisions in God's will too. But they were all just faithfully prayed about and we moved on in our lives following God's will without laying out a fleece before God.

Now, it seemed that the only thing to do was to lay a "fleece of faith" before God to find his perfect will in the matter.

First of all, my heart was not into moving north away from Texas, Tennessee, South Carolina, or anywhere that wasn't in Southern territory below the Mason-Dixon line. One fact of faith fumble in my heart-my heart was not into taking a pastorate up north.

We agreed to go and preach in view of a call to become the pastor of this northern, county-seat church. It was a large church with a live radio program for the morning worship and had over three hundred people in Sunday School and about four hundred in worship. So it was a nice size church.

My fifth "fleece of faith" was:

"God, if you want me to become the pastor of this church then let someone get saved when I preach and let there be less than ten "no" votes for me to be the pastor by written ballot".

This was my simple fleece with my simple faith and complete trust in God for the outcome!

After I preached and gave the invitation, no one came down the aisle to make a decision. Actually, it seemed nobody even blinked or moved. So I felt part of my fleece was answered but now they were to vote on me to become their pastor by written ballot.

The chairman of the pulpit committee took our family out of the worship center and into the Pastor's office while the church conducted the vote. Well, after a seemingly long time, the Chairman and other committee members came into the office and said they had 286 yes votes and six no votes!

They were happy and excited and felt I would accept the Pastorate of the church. However, they did not know about my "fleece of faith," only half of my fleece had been answered in the assurance of God's perfect will for me in this matter.

I had to tell the committee to inform the church which was still in the Worship Center waiting for my answer, that I would need another week to pray to be sure of God's will.

Now our family was to go downstairs to the Fellowship Hall for a "special luncheon" with all the pulpit committee and officers of the church. It had been planned for our family to meet and greet them.

While we were sitting at the table, they had me sitting next to the Chairman of the Deacon Body. He leaned over and said to me, "When you left the worship center for the church to vote, a young married couple came forward and gave their life to Jesus Christ and were saved after you preached today's message."

Well, hallelujah and glory to God in the highest! God showed up and showed out again in his mighty and miraculous way. He had answered my fifth major "fleece of faith."

It was definitely answered but God took his time in getting me the answer for his will. Remember I did not want to go to this church. It was a must for God to truly direct my way and to answer my fleece and he did!

(Note: Tell about all the success here before my "faith fumble.") We really enjoyed God's will and blessings in being the pastor of this rather large and beautiful First Baptist Church. It was one of the best in our immediate area, mainly because we were in the county-seat town.

We surely had God's hand of blessings on the ministry for we began to grow quickly in all areas of the church aged from preschool through the oldest senior adults! We led our state for two years in growth attendance in Sunday School until we were over five hundred and over six hundred in worship.

In one revival week that I preached on the concluding service, I had the happy honor of baptizing thirty-eight people at one time. Most of these were young adults and older teenagers. The church sure had God's hand upon all we did and as the Book of Nehemiah says, "The people had a heart to work."

As it always happens, the devil causes problems within a growing church to try and stop God's blessings and progress.

There is no need to go into all the reasons for my "faith fumble" during this time, but it was a very tough time of spiritual warfare (Ephesians 6:10–19).

I truly went into a "spiritual burnout" time in my life. Mostly, it was a time of carelessness by me not to remember the devil is like a roaring lion seeking who he can devour." (1 Peter 5:8).

The next chapter will continue this situation

CHAPTER 8

God's Gunslinger
(1979–1997)

It was June of 1979 and it would be one of the hottest summers on record as we continue the "faith fumble" of the last chapter.

I resigned from this church with absolute "spiritual burn out". I had no direction for what I was going to do. After all the success and the blessings in this church, I was just ready to completely give up being in the ministry and serving God! It was all my failure and fault!

If I were to continue in the ministry, God was going to have to show me and direct me. I was like the prophet Jonah, I was in rebellion to God and ready to quit.

It was June 1979, I had resigned from the church and we had nowhere to go, no money on hand or in savings, and no direction of what to do at all for our life and the future!

I decided to take my family and drive to Tennessee to some beloved friends who had become like a mom and dad to me through the last ten years of my life from my very first pastorate while in college.

It was at their house in the beautiful hills of East Tennessee that my next "fleece of faith" was laid before God. It would be my sixth major fleece in my life seeking God's divine direction!

Here was my simple fleece:

"God, I don't know what to do! Please direct me and show me what you'd have me do for your Will in my life. Please, by July 4th, about three days from now, show me what you want me to do. Make it a direct opportunity for me to minister or I will leave the ministry and get a job in the business world."

(Note: I had decided to move my family to the Greenville/Spartanburg area of South Carolina and just seek employment there. Mainly because I had friends there and I liked the area which was growing with people, jobs, industries.)

Remember I had asked God to answer my fleece before midnight on July 3, just three days away! Again, the unexpected happened! Keep in mind that no one knew my fleece, except me, my wife, and my heavenly Father God!

Oh, I had told my friends we were staying with that we were thinking of moving down to South Carolina or even back to East Tennessee. However, we did not tell them of the "fleece of faith' I had laid before God!

Yes, again the unexpected and most unusual happened from God, and the answer divinely and directly came from God's hand.

It came as a phone call from a man out of Dallas, Texas. He had a relative in the church up north I had pastored and recently left. He wanted me to immediately return his telephone call. This was still two days before my fleece would expire at midnight on July 3.

Remember, I'd never heard of this man nor ever met him! When I called him, he was in Dallas and I was in East Tennessee, he bluntly said, "Ted Padgett, I've never met you, and yet I've heard how greatly God has used you in the church you've just resigned. God has placed you in my heart to offer you a ministry position with me in serving the Lord. Would you come and talk with me about it?"

Wow, hallelujah and praise the Lord! God had answered again in his mighty and miraculous way in my life and in answering my "fleece of faith"!

We were to meet halfway between Knoxville, Tennessee, and Dallas, Texas. He said to meet him the next evening for dinner in Memphis, Tennessee, at the Airport Holiday Inn at 5:00 p.m. He said he'd have a room reserved for my family.

All went as God planned for our lives through this man of faith. He did offer me the executive position in his ministry that was based out of Dallas, Texas. We did know it was God's will and accepted the position.

Again, my "fleece of faith" had been divinely and directly answered by God. He certainly has had patience with me in my life of service for him.

The next series of events in our life was moving our family to Dallas, Texas. By the way, this is an interesting story of how God led and blessed us in our moving. We joined the First Baptist Church of Dallas where the great legend, Dr. W.A. Criswell, became our pastor during the next five years.

It was a great time of being used in ministry without all the pressures and concerns that had previously caused my "spiritual burnout" and my faith fumble in ministry! Dr. Criswell was my pastor and mentor during these years of refreshing, resting, and renewal in ministry.

Many great things happened in these five years at Dallas. Let me name some of these for you to see how God was using our family in the ministry. We were led to start a church and eventually First Baptist Church of Dallas took it over as we got it chartered and established.

I was used all over the country to preach, speak, and help churches grow in the ministry that God had placed me in and preached many revivals and led conferences for evangelism. It was a great time for me and, above all, for my family to strengthen our bond of spiritual unity.

After these years of ministry, home-based in Dallas, we were called back to east Tennessee to pastor a medium sized church. We would spend the next twelve years in this sweet church of very beloved and precious people.

It was during this pastorate and time of my life's ministry that I became known as "God's gunslinger." Here is the story of how that nickname came to be.

One early morning, I drove up to the church where I was pastoring and arrived before anyone had gotten there first, for the day's work. As I pushed the outside door open, I noticed that we had been broken into because the office window was broken

Since I'd been in the military, as the early chapters stated, I still practiced with my rifle and my pistol which was in the trunk of my car. I went back to my car and got my pistol. Going back into the church office area with pistol in hand, two men came out of one of our offices with a typewriter and other equipment.

Immediately, I pointed my gun on them and told them not to move, but one of them took off running down the church hallway. The other is where I kept my gun on and led him outside. Also, by now, the church's custodian had arrived and I asked her to call the police. I took the man outside and got his identity out of his wallet—it was a prison parole card. He had been in prison for robbery and murder!

The police then came and took him off to jail and eventually back to prison. However, newspapers and TV made a big deal of a local pastor catches robber, calling me "God's gunslinger." Even the American Rifle Association Magazine did a small article and called me the same name. By the way, later that year, I wrote a book entitled *God's Gunslinger,* which was about evangelism in America.

The twelve years that I pastored this church in East Tennessee was a wonderful time in our lives—for the church and my family.

These twelve years at this church saw multiple blessings from God on our ministry. The church experienced growth in numbers and spiritual maturity. This church would, in later years, name me their Pastor Emeritus.

It was the fall of 1996. So many things had happened in our lives and ministry.

(See: *Changed* by Ted O. Padgett, 2018)

However, this book is about the fleece and the seven major fleeces of my life. Keep in mind that seven is God's perfect number, and that's why I've decided to use seven major "fleeces of faith" in my life to show the fact of faith of the fleece laid before God!

Now the next chapter will give the seventh major "Fleece of Faith" in my life

CHAPTER 9

Building and Battling
(1997–2012)

So, Gideon laid a fleece before God to determine God's will.
- Judges 6:36-40 (Paraphrased, NRSV)

It was the late fall of 1996 when a church down in Georgia began to write, telephone, and communicate with me that they believed God wanted me to become their pastor. It was a church in the Atlanta area, approximately thirty miles southwest from downtown Atlanta. By the way, it had to be God's will because I loved where we were, and it had been twelve years.

(Note: All our four children were gone from home. They were either married and/or in college full-time by the fall of 1996. Also, my wife and I had reached the age of fifty. My wife had always wanted to be a nurse before we got married, but she became the mother of four children.)

Now that the children were grown and gone, I encouraged her to follow her dream of becoming a nurse. She did, and at the age of fifty-four, she graduated top in her class with an LPN degree! She would graduate the first Friday of March 1997. That's important because I had accepted the Georgia church's call to be their pastor in January 1997.

We were waiting for my wife to graduate from nursing school in March before moving to Georgia to begin our ministry. We decided to officially begin on the last Sunday of March 1997, which would be Easter Sunday. So on Easter Sunday of 1997, we began this new pastorate in Georgia.

We would be at this church for sixteen years. This would be a time of building and battling". Much of this time would be a time of "spiritual warfare"; however, this would become another very beloved place and people.

After my sixteen years there and retiring from ministry, they would also make me their Pastor Emeritus.

This seventh major "fleece of faith" for my life would come after about five years into my time as pastor of this church. Let me set the stage and/or give you the setting and background for my seventh major fleece.

From the very beginning of my ministry at this church, it was a tough spiritual warfare time of "building and battling" for God's glory (See: Book of Nehemiah and Ephesians 6:10–19). It all started because we had "boss deacon" at the church who did not understand that the pastor is God's leader of the flock.

There were twelve deacons serving this church as it's boss. There was a dad, two of his sons, and two sons-in-law in the twelve. So one family had five of the twelve deacons—the oldest, the dad-was the real "boss deacon."

Immediately in 1997, it was my task to change the *deacon* concept of "boss deacons"! I changed the term they used of "Deacon Board" to the term "Deacon Body". Of course, rebellion and opposition began.

(Note: The blessing of God had so fallen upon our ministry at this church by the spring of 2001, and no one could doubt that God's hand and blessings were upon me and our ministry of spiritual and numerical growth.)

My wife and I endured ugly letters, secret meetings to get rid of me, untrue stories, flat lies about me, and ugly letters to the member ship. To top it all, a meeting was called for me to meet with one of the main leaders of the spiritual opposition against me.

He was a self-made millionaire in our church membership, one of the former "boss deacons." (By the way, God had sent a great and godly deacon chairman to our church in 1998, and he served as the chairman of the Deacon Body by my side and for God's glory from 1998-2012 when I would retire after approximately sixteen years of ministry at this church.)[17]

He would be by my side and with me as my great friend and helper, counselor, and negotiator through all the ugly actions of these corrupt and carnal Christians during the attacks against me and our ministry. All I was doing was preaching and teaching the Bible.

Anyway, the deacon chairman and I met in my pastor's office with this corrupt and carnal former church deacon. Remember, he was a self-made millionaire and thought he was a *real somebody*, and he *tooted his horn*, boosting his importance and everything else.

Oh, his worldly wife was the *wicked witch of the west*. In other words, she was mostly at the center of the storm. In fact, she kept the fires and ugly letters going about me to our membership. So to get the picture clear, this deacon asked for me to meet with him in my pastor's office at the church! Well, unknown to him, I asked my faithful and godly chairman of our Deacon Body to go to this meeting with me.

As the three of us met in my office, the millionaire deacon sat there and said to me, "Pastor Ted, I am willing to give you $100,000 to resign and leave this church." Well, to me, this was the last straw. I told him to get out and that he and his money would be cursed by God for him to have even offered such a thing. He left in a huff, angry as could be.

This horrible act and the pressure of all the ugly acts against me brought me to my seventh major "fleece of faith" for God's will and divine direction! Remember, I had been here since 1997 until 2001, about five years.

"God, show me your perfect Will for my life. God, I am going to call for a written ballot vote for me to continue as Pastor of this church. Let the vote of the people clearly show that you are with me and want me as the Pastor. Make the vote so overwhelming it will be clear to all the church members.

Now let me give you some background behind the scenes of the time that I set up the "special vote."

First of all, only my most trusted spiritual helpers or "spiritual warriors" were going to know about the "special vote." It was in my heart from God to let no one know how and when the vote would take place.

God led me to have the Moderator for the Association of our church come and moderate and lead in the "special vote" about me and the pastorate. Then with the deacons involved, we set the "special vote" to be conducted on a Sunday night.

This was to be a once and for all vote to keep me as the pastor. I had served for five and a half years at this time. Also, it was to be a final call for all the disgruntled, objective, and critical people to get on board with our church or to leave immediately if I had a vote of 80 percent.

On the night of the vote, I'd planned to go to Dallas, Texas, and spend that weekend with my son. Only our deacon chairman knew I had planned to be gone, except I told the association moderator to conduct the special meeting and vote. It would be a complete surprise for me not to be there.

Well, the vote was taken, and I won by a 90 percent of the votes of those who voted by secret written ballot! What a joy and blessing when, after the vote, the chairman of the deacons called me with the news of the positive vote!

This was April 2001, and the real ugly leaders and a few of their critical followers left the church. The church once again grew in numbers and new converts.

Fast forward to September of 2012. This would be seven and a half years later, and the Lord led me to retire from active ministry and return to my home in East Tennessee. I'd pastored this church for over fifteen years. It was a time of "building and battling" in spiritual warfare for God's glory!

When my wife and I finally left this church, it was a time of joy and sadness because we had grown to love the people and place.

The ministry of my wife had been a time of serving very close to our home as a school nurse where she had a job, but even more so, a ministry to the school staff and the school's children.

We both knew God had been with us during those fifteen and a half years at our places of service that God had called us to serve. We can only say, "To do what God desires as his perfect will always bring joy and fulfillment knowing you are in God's will for your life."

CHAPTER 10

Be Believing
(2012–2018)

So, Gideon laid a fleece before God to determine God's will.

- Judges 6:36-40 (Paraphrased, NRSV)

This book started with a chapter about dealing with the doubters and skeptics many of whom are scholars and trained Bible Theologians. My hope in sharing my belief and seven of my major fleeces of my life is to show God does answer the fleece, and not just for Gideon, but any believing person of faith.

The use of the fleece to seek God's will is an act of believing faith in God. You must believe that God hears your fleece and will answer it.

Remember in the Gospel of John, chapter 20, Jesus shares a wonderful fact about believing faith (see John 20:24–29). Jesus told Thomas in verse 27, "Do not be unbelieving but believing," as a fact of faith!

Then Thomas answered and said in verse 28, "My Lord and my God!"

In verse 29, Jesus makes a bedrock statement of believing faith.

He says, "Thomas, because you have seen me, you have believed. Blessed are those who have not seen and yet have believed."

It is by faith that we are saved and not works or any other way (see Ephesians 2:8-10). We must remember what God's Word has taught us, that it is "faith that pleases God." It is a major factor in using the "fleece of faith." You must be earnestly seeking God's divine will to lay a fleece before God, asking him to lead, guide, and direct you.

It is important to remember that you do not and cannot use the "fleece of faith" for every little trivial whim or desire you want answered by God or every decision you make. Prayer, "spiritual praying," is always a must in the life of a believer. However, the "fleece of faith" can be used for major decisions of a life-changing direction and decision.

(Note: The seven major fleeces of my life are shared to help show you can use the fleece as Gideon did to make absolute certain of God's will.)

We must remember what the Word of God says in many places about God giving us guidance and direction. As in Proverbs 3:6, it says, "In all your ways, acknowledge him, and he shall direct your paths."

Your great desire in life should be to know God's will for your life, and your great delight in life should be to do God's will. Your greatest danger and disappointment in life is to refuse God's will. As I close this book on the "fleece of faith" or subtitle "How to Find God's Will," let me give some myths concerning the will of God that I have learned along my spiritual journey. Some of these have come from my own personal sermons or from others I've gleaned from in my years of being a student and/or minister.

First is what I call the Map Myth. The Map Myth is that God is going to give you a road map for his will for you. The will of God is not a road map, it is a relationship with him as a believer.

Second is the Misery Myth. It is the belief that if you do the will of God, it will be painful and will make you full of misery. For example, if some feel that if I do God's will, he's going to send me to the jungles of Africa away from my loved ones.

Third is the Miracle Myth. This myth states that you must have something dramatic to know God's will for your life. In this, you must have some miraculous sign to always point you to God's will. This is not like a "fleece of faith" where you need to make sure of his will and by believing by faith you lay a fleece before God (see Judges 6:36-40)

Remember, God may speak to you in a miracle or a sign, but generally he does not.

(For example, see 1 Kings 19:11–12).

Fourth is the Missionary Myth, to which many feel that God only calls a certain class of people. This Missionary Myth concept of knowing God's will is a belief that unless you are a certain class of people. This, of course, is *not* true because God has a plan and a will for everyone!

Lastly, there is the Mystery Myth, which is a belief about knowing God's will for your life. It simply means that God has a plan for your life but that you must search and hunt for it. It is like an Easter egg hunt. Our great God truly wants you to know his will and do it for his honor and glory. (See Psalm 37:23.)

There are three great facts of faith in finding God's will for your life that you must know and understand. God has a "prevailing will," a "permissive will," and a "personal will" that must be understood to help in using a "fleece of faith" to know God's personal will for your life.

First, God's prevailing will means that his great sovereign purpose can never be ultimately thwarted or overthrown. God's sovereign will is going to be done with his creation and plan for the ages.

Second, God's permissive will means that God has a general will. For example, man has a free will to do as he desires. God does not make us robots where we must do his will; it is our free choice. God permits this!

Third, God's personal will means that God has a will and plan for each one of us. He has many plans as he has many people. God is interested in each individual. The Bible goes as far as to say, "The very hairs of your head are all numbered" (Matthew 10:30).

God has a personal will for every believer.

Remember, it takes a devout faith to use the "fleece of faith." So you ask, what is believing faith and what is faith?

At the very basic, faith is simply trusting and obeying."

This is what really pleases God. Romans 10:17 says, "Faith comes by hearing and the hearing of God's Word." All true faith in

God is rooted not only in knowing God, but in hearing from the God that you know!

Remember, we do not use the "fleece of faith" in every situation but only in major life "directional decisions" from God.

So we must remember that God speaks to us and directs us by believing faith daily.

How does God communicate his word to us today? It is by his

Word and hearing it that we have faith and grow in our faith. (See Romans 10:11-17.)

There are two words used for "word" in the Bible; one is the Greek word *logos*, which means the written Word. The other is *rhema,* which means a spoken word or an utterance proclaimed. We call it in theological terms "a word from the Word."

So how does God speak to us today? It is by reading and/or hearing His Word, the *logos*, and receiving a word (the *rhema)* to us personally—his personal word to us!

It is by this fact of faith that we do not have to use a "fleece of faith' at every intersection and/or crossroad of our life.

It is my hope and personal desire that all who read this book will believe in the fact of the "fleece of faith." Remember, God's Word is truth, and nothing will be void in his Word. The Bible says:

"So, Gideon laid a fleece before God to determine God's will for his life" (Judges 6:36-40, NRSV).[18]

NOTES

1. MacArthur, John. *Found: God's will.* Colorado: David C. Cook Publishers, 1977.
2. Bargerhuff, Eric J. *The Most Misused Stories in the Bible.* Minnesota: Bethany House Publishers, 2017.
3. Phillips, W. Gary. *Holman Old Testament Commentary.* Judges, Vol. 5, pp. 91–106. Tennessee: B&H Publishing Group, 2004.
4. (This central thesis will be seen in the story of my life and the major areas given to help show this fact.)
5. Wiersbe, Warren W. *Judges: Be Available* (pp. 68–69). Old Testament Commentary, Colorado: David C. Cook Publishers, 1994.
6. (These are the principles for using the "fleece of faith" and the book's central thesis.)
7. Graham, Frank. *Rebel with a Cause.* Tennessee: Thomas Nelson, Inc., 1995.
8. (This story shares that he and his father used the fleece, Gideon seeking God's will to be certain. This is recorded in the Bible, Judges 6:36-40.)
9. Padgett, Ted O. *Home Sweet Home* (pp. 7–30). Oklahoma: Spirit Publications, 1987.
10. (John's Gospel, chapter 3, Jesus is explaining to Nicodemus about salvation and the Kingdom of God.) (See John 3:1-21.)
11. (Read the autobiography, *Changed,* written by Ted O. Padgett [AN-TOP Publishers, TOP Ministries, Seymour, Tennessee, 2018]. My life and the similar story of Franklin Graham's life as shared in his book, *Rebel with a Cause.*)
12. (The title came from 2 Corinthians 5:17.)

13. (Bart Easter was my spiritual mentor, my Sunday School teacher and lifelong friend. J. Walker Campbell was my pastor at First Baptist Church of San Diego, California, 1965.)
14. (Jeremiah 1:4–9 and many other places show God's call to people for his divine service. This was a preparation time in my life for future days of ministry and service. The church that called me as their interim pastor/preacher for Sundays was the First Baptist Church of La Mesa, California. I very much enjoyed that time/experiences.)
15. (Judges 6:36-40, Gideon's request to God for his direction. He knew God's will but was still unsure.)
16. (The Bible says in Hebrews 11:6, "It is faith that pleases God and without faith we cannot please Him.")
17. (Gene Holbrook was my great friend and the chairman of the Deacon Body, 1999-2012. He has been my great spiritual friend.)
18. Many thanks to my daughter, Deanna Padgett Sexton, for typing my rough manuscript into a computer smooth copy. She helped her "Papa" to complete this manuscript.

BIBLIOGRAPHY

Bargerhuff, Eric J. The Most Misused Stories in the Bible. Minnesota: Bethany House Publishers, 2017.

Block, Daniel I. The New American Commentary, Volume 6, Judges & Ruth. Tennessee: B & H Publishing Group, 1999.

Bowling, R.G. Judges. New Jersey: Doubleday Publishers, 1975.

Graham, Franklin. Rebel with A Cause. Tennessee: Thomas Nelson Publisher, 1995.

Harrison, Roland K. Introduction to the Old Testament, Michigan: Eerdmans Publishers, 1969.

Inrig, Gary, Hearts of Iron, Feet of Clay (Judges). Chicago: Moody Press, 1979.

Lindsey, Duane F. Judges. The Bible Knowledge Commentary, Old Testament, Edited by John F. Walvood and Roy B. Zuck. Illinois: Victor Books, 1985.

MacArthur, John. Found: God's will. Colorado: David C. Cook Publishers, 1977.

Padgett, Ted O. Evangelism in America Since 1700. Tennessee: AN-TOP Publishers, 1972.

Padgett, Ted O. Home Sweet Home. Oklahoma: Spirit Publications, 1987,

Padgett, Ted O. God's Gunslinger. Oklahoma: Spirit Publications, 1989.

Slotki, Judah J. Judges, Introduction and Commentary, The Soncino Books of the Bible, Edited by A. Cohen. London: The Soncino Press, 1950.

Wiersbe, Warren W. Judges: Be Available, Old Testament Commentary. Colorado: David C. Cook Publishers, 1994.

Wood, Leon, The Distressing Days of the Judges. Michigan: Zondervan Publishers, 1975.